fantasies
& games
for lovers

fantasies
& games
for lovers

paul scott

illustrations by pinglet@pvuk.com

RYLAND
PETERS
& SMALL

LONDON NEW YORK

Senior Designer **Paul Tilby**
Editor **Miriam Hyslop**
Production **Gavin Bradshaw**
Art Director **Gabriella Le Grazie**
Publishing Director **Alison Starling**

Illustrations **pinglet@pvuk.com**

First published in the
United States in 2005
by Ryland Peters & Small, Inc.
519 Broadway
5th Floor
New York, NY 10012
www.rylandpeters.com

10 9 8 7 6 5 4 3

ISBN-10: 1-84172-790-3
ISBN-13: 978-1-84172-790-5

contents

introduction

Why we have fantasies, and why sex games are fun

Even at its most normal and everyday, the world of human sexuality is always a little absurd. Advertising and culture tell us all that certain ways of looking and being—a woman's slim hips, pert bottom, big breasts; a man's thick hair, broad chest, and ample penis—are desirable, while others are less so. However, we are all individuals, and these aspects that are supposed to be universally desired are, in fact, not universal at all. Ideas of beauty are different in different times and cultures, and they obscure the reality that we are most truly aroused by individuals in themselves.

Everyone is different, and it's the various differences that draw us to one person over another. However, there's always more to learn about the person you've chosen—thank goodness, or relationships would grow more stale much more quickly—and some of a person's most hidden thoughts are sexual ones. Threesomes; being dominated; having anonymous sex, forced sex, or making love with a celebrity; watching your partner with another lover; messy, naughty fun or kinky pleasure and pain; all of these and more are common elements of the normal sexual fantasies that most people have.

Don't be ashamed of them—having sexual fantasies does not necessarily mean you want to act them out. Beliefs that it is wrong to have sexual fantasies went along with a belief in the harmful effects of masturbation. And thanks to medical science we now know that there aren't any. In fact, sexual fantasy can give a voice to deeply repressed fears, so it's not only fun, it's a necessary part of working out our lives. Sometimes an idea alone resonates with us strongly enough to arouse us. At other times, physical arousal—whether during lovemaking or, more inexplicably, when we're alone—encourages us to take our minds to a fantasy space.

Events in our sexual imagination always go the way we want them to, and most people know there's a difference between fantasy and reality. It helps to understand the difference if we can exchange our sexual fantasies with our lover. This doesn't have to be the ghastly and serious process it sounds, however, and it's only as clinical as you want it to be. Remember, you don't have to tell them everything, and you may be pleasantly surprised by how much your fantasies chime with theirs.

The bad news is that your lover will not be fantasizing about you all the time. All the more incentive, then, to find out what makes your lover tick... Sharing your fantasies casually, playfully, and spontaneously requires and reinforces the trust that exists between you. Knowing what turns your partner on is incredibly arousing in itself, as well as making you a better lover—we like what we're good at, and we're good at what we like.

Simply knowing what your partner might be thinking about during sex is incredibly arousing by itself. The ideas and games in this book may help you tease those secret fantasies out of each other even further.

fantasies

telling stories

It's no coincidence that stories and bedtime have always gone together. It's often said that the brain is our most important sex organ, and with good reason. Nothing fuels our passions like sexual fantasy. Although couples who are able to share their sexual fantasies are very lucky, they are also not uncommon. Remember that you do not have to swap every last detail of your sexual fantasies, nor do you have to reveal all your fantasies to your lover—it's entirely a question of degree. It may help to think about how your fantasy character might behave in some of the more commonly imagined sexual scenarios that you might not have thought about before.

Many sexual fantasies come from history and Hollywood, and historical romances have been a staple of erotic fiction for years.

One such is the myth of piracy on the high seas. Imagine your partner as a swashbuckling pirate, or a maiden taken—or rescued—by them. Your story can be as simple as you like. Tell each other stories that feature the other as a character—your partner may be more impressed if you leave yourself out. Don't be afraid to think of dialogue for your characters—it speeds a story along and makes it more dynamic.

Have your characters tell your partner how sexy they are. This is an opportunity for you to impress your partner with how much you have been listening to them and absorbing what makes them tick. Think about what they have told you about what turns them on, and work it into your story. If they don't feel much like Keira Knightley, Johnny Depp, or Errol Flynn when you start, they may by the end.

fireman's lift

The perfect combination of assertiveness and sensitivity is wonderfully arousing to a lover of either sex. As partners, all of us can be insecure about how much we measure up to the romantic and fantasy images our partner has, but much is to be gained from simply showing them we want to.

Learn to judge your lover's mood and take seduction slowly—it's role-play in itself. There's nothing sexier to many men than a woman who knows what she wants behind that respectable, perhaps slightly embarrassed veneer, and there's nothing sexier to most women than a lover whose charm and support masks his insatiable need to have her.

Why not think about exploring these themes with your partner. Strong but kind, they will take no for an answer, but be bold enough to have a go, all measured charm and civility as they put their hand on your thigh. What roles in life reflect the character type you find attractive? What sexual positions give you a sense of their tender power? Not all uniformed fantasy figures are about submission and domination—some simply come to your emotional rescue.

exhibitionism

If you enjoy the idea of showing off for your lover, you're not alone. Exhibitionistic behavior is the opposite of furtive voyeurism. Just as there are those who like to watch, there are those that like to be watched—in fact, driving men wild with exhibitionistic displays is, according to some surveys, the number one female fantasy.

In reaction to the in-your-face nature of much cheaply available pornography, the seductive arts of striptease and burlesque dancing—with their feather boas and leopard-print bikinis—are making a comeback. So instead of thinking about revealing yourself to that soft rock ballad, you could think in terms of a beat combo soundtrack.

If the idea of arousing others turns you on, you may well be aware that men and women both report equally that a partially naked body is often far sexier than a completely naked one. If you put your striptease fantasy into action, then, without looking like you're off to the North Pole, the more clothes you start with, the better. Give yourself plenty of things to undo in the way of buckles, clips, straps, and laces, and you will enhance the sense of anticipation. Mood is everything, so soft lighting and a relaxed space are essential. Equally, formal clothes can also make for a sexy strip, as the contrast between your assumed propriety and your decadent delight will be all the greater.

open air

For some extra-naughty—or extra-spiritual—arousal, show some
skin and take your lovemaking outside, taking due care of the law
and public decency. Although it's not fashionable to say so, the
sensation of sunshine on your skin will increase your libido.
Expose yourself to the life-giving rays of the sun. Find secluded
places in a beautiful wilderness, get lost in the long grass and
really get away from it all. Or else stay at home on a sunny day,
and make love beneath the sill of a window, as shafts of light
stream in.

One cool position in particular is perfect for hot sex in the sunshine: the woman lies on
her back on top of her lover's chest. He may need a hand to enter her, and penetration
will be shallow. But she can luxuriate in the sunlight on her breasts, belly, and clitoris, all
of which are accessible to both their hands. And, if she lies with her head back, she can
listen to the sweet nothings he can whisper in her ear. Placing her feet flat on the floor or
ground, and pushing up a little, will give you both a little more movement. A palm on the
base of his shaft from either of you will allay his fears about popping out.

thrills

to enhance your mood

★ *Provided your partner's not allergic, flowers— especially colorful, large and fragrant ones—are bound to provide them with a frisson of romance. You needn't restrict them to a vase; sprinkle flowers in the bathtub, too.*

★ *Don't forget the power of Mother Nature. A breathtaking mountain top, a sunset at the beach, cool, running water... natural wonders are the most romantic there are. But don't forget a blanket—cold will soon bring you back down to earth.*

★ Seduction is not a by-numbers ritual. If you've fallen into a pattern, do it in reverse order.

★ You can never have too many pillows and cushions, either for relaxing, or supporting your bodies in various sexual positions. Keep plenty around your bed, and simply toss them aside if they're in the way.

★ Candles are a cliché but for good reason. The right lighting is essential. Uplighting or shaded lighting is better than harsh overhead light every time.

★ Treat your partner to a bath. The simple act of running or drawing it for them is easily achieved and yet a clear signal that you want them to relax.

costumes

The idea of dressing for sex is nothing new: the Ancient Greeks enjoyed licentious festivals of Saturnalia, while in eighteenth-century London the young and trendy attended all-night masquerades, where masks added intrigue, and clothes were fantastical, mythological, and transgressive.

These days, we're familiar with the fetish wear that is available in sex stores, sold to be worn both as club wear and in the bedroom, and we all understand the sexual signal of erotic lingerie. If, however, the idea of dressing up in a costume makes you feel a little absurd or self-conscious, then don't forget that dressing for sex can involve our everyday clothes, too. If we're honest, then, like Bridget Jones's "big knickers," there will be something our partner wears which does it for us, even though they may not have a clue. "Fetish wear" is a marketing term that obscures the fact that every item or style of clothing is sexualized by someone, somewhere.

Your partner could be a parking attendant, a waitress, or a cop. Many clothes are sexy for the roles they convey, and uniforms—although we may not think of them as such—often become popular dressing up costumes for this reason. Overlapping with this is the way that we find clothing sexy because of its tailoring—the way in which it hugs or falls away from your lover's body. Anything could be a costume. It could be a powerful-looking business suit, or a flattering pair of shorts. If you find yourself aroused by something your partner wears as part of their everyday lives, then for goodness' sake tell them—it's perfectly normal.

courtly love

Even though many of us may not have been inclined to listen intently at school, there's no doubt that English literature has always reflected and inspired sexual fantasies. It started in the twelfth century, at the flirtatious court of Eleanor of Aquitaine and Henry II. While crusading knights put their feet up with heroic Norse sagas as if they were Tom Clancy stories, their wives were excited by romantic tales of courtly love, told by seductive troubadours, which were the "chick-lit" of their day.

The knights in these stories weren't short of dragon-slaying power, but when it came to love, they were in thrall to their ladies as if they were their "liege lords." The women were on top—often married—and when the knights couldn't court them, they expressed their love with brave deeds instead.

Women writers of the nineteenth century such as Jane Austen and Charlotte Brontë presented men as lust objects, whose feral, beast-like instincts are sometimes barely constrained by social manners as tight as Mr. Darcy's breeches. Images such as Darcy and Heathcliff persist throughout romantic literature and erotic novels, but in the beginning they were well-rounded characters, too.

Twentieth-century stories from *Valley of the Dolls*, through novels like *The Bitch*, to the light-hearted approach of Jilly Cooper's novels, often inhabit the same world as those tales of courtly love, in which powerful men are helplessly enslaved by seductive women. So when it comes to understanding some of the strange, arousing puzzles of human sexuality, we can do a lot worse than curling up with a good book.

medication time

"Ooh, nurse! Oh, doctor!"—medical scenes are role-play favorites among fetishists, while humorous references to medical staff as sex objects have filled popular culture since the 1940s. There are powerful reasons why nurses and doctors have been the objects of our lusts: not only is it natural to desire those fine, upstanding people who give of their training and expertise in the name of humanity, but then there's those crisp, rustling coats and uniforms and plenty of opportunities for power-play. Perhaps they have made such an impression on us because our earliest memories are often of trauma, usually in hospital, while many children experience the distress of injury or illness made better by medical mercy, and we sexualize our vivid, fearful times as a coping mechanism.

You don't have to get too physically invasive to enjoy some clinically themed fun with your lover. It's the perfect opportunity for a little anticipation, expectation, and playful control. Affordable toy stethoscopes, disposable rubber gloves, and plastic sheeting will give you a sense of contrasting sensations (chill some accessories in the fridge or reach for some ice to "numb" the area under treatment), and will give you the perfect opportunity to boss your lover around, making them love and fear you; or to pamper them and allow them to luxuriate in your nurturing touch.

thrills

to make your body tingle I

★ *Involve all of your lover's senses, and don't neglect touch, taste, and smell: scented massage oil, ice, honey, mangoes... add to the sight and sound of sex in whatever way you like.*

★ *Men, if your lover already owns a vibrator or a dildo, ask her to show or tell you how she uses it, then use it on her in the way she likes during lovemaking. Don't be limited by thinking you can only use it like a penis—this one is detached.*

★ Bring one of your lover's nipples to the height of arousal, caress and feather it with your fingers and tongue-tip. Just when they're expecting you to close upon it, slide over to the other, leaving it tingling for more.

★ Anal play doesn't have to be an all-or-nothing proposition involving penetration: you can lovingly explore the surface of an anus with kisses, licks, and strokes, and see where that leads you.

★ Neglect the nubs of your lover's nipples in favor of ringing their areola with your tongue or fingers—they may be dark as coffee or nearly non-existent, but these haloes of pleasure can be filled with more nerve endings than the tips themselves.

★ A partner of either sex will love having their perineum (the spot between their genitals and anus) rubbed with firm, circular motions during intercourse.

assume the position

In recent decades, fetish fashion found its way onto international catwalks, pop stars modeled corsets and high heels which were copied by major clothing stores, and films and videos have featured no end of rubber and leather wear. Debate raged about whether these figures—usually women—were empowered icons or slaves to fashion. Some women say that dressing for sex is making yourself too available, reinforcing sexual objectification; others, that they feel a corset or costume only reinforces their own sense of strength and attractiveness. Perhaps the only way is to try it, and find out how you feel.

One thing's for sure: women have sexual fantasies that revolve around role-play, submission, domination, bondage, and sado-masochism just as much as men do, perhaps even with more elaboration. And when it comes to acting these out, the dominant partner of either sex is really being submissive, because they are trying, however perversely, to please their lover, who is meanwhile soaking up sensation. So don't be confused or ashamed if, in your fantasies, you find yourself controlled, on the losing side, surrendering power. True personal strength, for people of either sex, is to be found in self-expression.

office junior

Whether it's a telling-off, or an interview, you'd be surprised to find how many of us fantasize about powerful experiences in the workplace. Whether it's white- or blue-collar, power arouses us, so workplace scenarios are perfect for power games, too. Whether you lust after a sharp-suited businessman who's in control, or a lady powerbroker who shakes down her hair after hours, the chances are you have real people in mind.

Bring this fantasy to your partner. Wear your smartest clothes, with your sexiest underwear underneath. Be the thrusting, dynamic achiever who gets what they want, or the retiring, nervous interviewee if you prefer—whichever you're least like, as a rule.

And if you have a home office, you don't have to worry about clearing the dining table, or risk sneaking your partner into the workplace after hours.

thrills

to make your body tingle II

★ *Try massaging each other's temples during long, slow, intimate, face-to-face sex. An ancient shiatsu technique, relaxing the face will relax other parts of the body and allow you to refocus on your arousal subsequently.*

★ *Give your lover a Thai massage. As a novice, you won't help their muscle tone, but you might turn them on. A large bathroom is best. Lying on towels, lather yourselves liberally with soap and water. The person giving the massage supports their own body weight, but rolls their body along their partner's.*

★ Feathers are fabulous for lovers who like to tease and tickle. They're sometimes the safest way to walk the fine line between pleasure and pain.

★ Kinky fabric materials like rubber and plastic are non-porous. It takes some talcum powder to get them on but many people report being aroused by the sweat and pheromones released.

★ Meanwhile, for a cheaper thrill, you could try liquid Latex, which shrinks to the body as it dries, or bondage tape, which sticks only to itself and makes a great restraint or blindfold.

★ Men, strange as it may sound, you can last longer during lovemaking by clenching your anus as tightly as you can when you feel you're not far from coming. The action translates directly to your hard-to-feel P.C. (pubococcygeus) muscle.

games

mind games

Most people have tried kinky sex of one form or another. You can take a hands-on approach, working various techniques, props, and gear into your foreplay. Or, between you, you could agree an entirely psychological one. When it comes to role-play, it's amazing how turned on some people are by the right combination of words, phrases, and attitudes once you take the plunge and try.

Communication is vital—no one expects you to read their mind. For goodness' sake, ask if you're not sure that what you're doing is lighting your lover's fire. Discuss boundaries not in the light of what you both fantasize about, but about when to halt—once you've visualized how it will really feel. Agree a "stop" word so that "no" doesn't have to mean "no", which can lead to confusion—selecting a "halt" word that's completely unerotic is best.

If you're interested in power-play, think what words, phrases, and attitudes really do it for you both before you get to physical contact or restraint—either in private, or maybe, for an extra thrill, with a private meaning when in public. Think about expressing yourself with your clothing, too. You may have always fancied keeping house as a saucy French maid, behaving like a dashing army officer, or teasing like a burlesque stripper. Pastiche is the name of the game, until you can't control your real selves any longer.

furniture testers

If you're looking to take sex beyond the bedroom, then take a new look at those familiar pieces of furniture—chairs, tables, and counters. Chairs hold limitless possibilities for tying your lover up, opening them to your tender mercies, or teasing them to distraction. Alternatively, the added range of penetrative sensations that having sex on a chair brings, compared to on a bed, is sure to broaden your possibilities. You may not both want to come in every possible position, so use them as foreplay on your way to the bedroom, if you prefer.

She might enjoy lowering herself onto his penis—he is already seated, and she sits on his erection. If she faces away from him, he can reach her clitoris and breasts, and nibble her ears. This is a great position for watching television together—especially a film that arouses you both. Alternatively, if she faces him, you have a great position for quickie sex.

A table or a counter at waist-height will give him somewhere to put her down when he needs a rest during those manly sessions where he stands and takes her weight. With her buttocks cradled in his hands or resting on the lip of a surface at the right height, she is in a perfect position to wrap her legs around him, her feet in the small of his back, drawing his hips towards her. Alternatively, she's in a great position on a kitchen surface, her labia open, for him to kneel and kiss the cook where it counts. Or take her out to the garage workbench, put on a mechanic's overall, and give her some lubrication.

grooming

Helping each other's grooming rituals is a natural, nurturing bonding practice that harks right back through human evolution. Some of us are a little bashful about sharing our deepest intimacies with our lover. If so, keep your distance when it counts—we're not suggesting that you let him pluck your chin hairs, or let her pluck your nose hair.

But helping your partner prepare themselves for the world can be a quietly helpful act that signals your support, making them feel strong at the beginning of the day, or more relaxed at the end of it. Men, paint your lover's toenails—slowly, carefully, and chattily—and see where it leads. Massage and worship her feet. Women, treat your man to a proper, old-time, wet shave (especially if you find stubble irritating either against your face or your genitals) a conventional bladed razor will do. Rest his head back, throw a towel around his neck, and whip up some lather—you don't have to sing. When you're done, caress his smoothened jaw. If you have the time, who knows how far you could take these grooming rituals?

private investigations

The following game provides a structure for getting
to know each other's responses a little better.

One of you takes charge, perhaps after an evening out, or an event you have shared
together. Set the scene, complete with candles and some mellow, sexy music. Ask your
lover to strip slowly and watch them, letting your gaze linger appreciatively on each area
of flesh that's revealed. The exhibitionist in them will find this really hot.

Strip off, too, if it makes them feel at ease, or else they might get a kick out of you being
clothed and dominant while they are naked and vulnerable. When they are naked, have
them lie down. Now it's time for you to undertake the most thorough investigation of their
pleasure centers they've ever had.

Start with your partner's neck, face, and ears, taking in every nook and cranny with your
tongue, lips, and fingertips. Give them a pleasure scale of one to ten. Ask them to score
how much pleasure they are getting from each place. Ask as you nibble and caress: "Do
you like having your neck bitten, like this?" "Do you like having your breasts licked...like this?"

Work your way down your lover's body from their temples to their toes and back again,
and don't miss a spot. Making a point of learning how to please your partner will impress
them no end, and could be the beginning of a very sensual relationship.

thrills

to make your mind reel

★ *Relax, don't do it! In getting carried away with your own pleasure, don't forget the value of a good tease. If you back off from whatever you're doing just as your partner's about to come, they won't thank you. However, a little earlier, and you'll have them begging for more.*

★ *If your lover's bashful about expressing their fantasies, get them to write down something lewd they'd like to do with you. Then you can get them to read it aloud.*

★ *Visit a gym together and put each other through your paces. It can be fun, rather than intimidating. Drink plenty of fluids. Have some covert sub–dom fun without other guests knowing, or simply get off on each other's tight clothes and natural scents.*

★ *Tie your partner's hands before you strip seductively for them. You'll be both submissive—exposing yourself for them—and dominant—restraining them. You'll also drive them wild with frustration.*

★ *If you both enjoy standing up for rear-entry sex, you can make your heads spin. Take it to new heights by doing it on a landing above a staircase, leaning over the banister as much as is safe and secure.*

★ *Take turns doing everything you tell each other to do, for an agreed period of time.*

toys

Not all games need toys, but many do. Vibrators and dildos are available in a range of styles, shapes, and sizes that vary far more widely than the human penis. Although many couples are put off by the noise, vibes have become quieter over the years as quality and materials have improved. Many now feature clitoral or anal stimulators, and separate power supplies. Although a vibrator will never mimic the motions of a real penis, more traditional models make great all-over massagers—don't forget nipples, the clitoris, and the skin of your lover's anal whorl.

Men—dildos and vibrators are your friends, not your rivals. They are another source of stimulation for her, or you. The best use of a vibrator is as a massager or dildo, while using a dildo can give your own penis somewhere else to go.

If the idea of a butt-plug seems a little daunting, then anal beads are a curious thrill. Make sure, however, never to insert anything into an anal passage that could disappear into the intestine. Anal beads should be connected to your finger by a cord. Use only butt-plugs with a recessed ring into which the sphincter can contract, holding them in place. When it comes to bondage, beware of cheap handcuffs, especially since they'll be the most widely available, sold in all sorts of novelty stores. Wide bands are preferable to thin, cutting cuffs. Far better to visit a reputable sex shop and take the assistant's advice as to the uses of custom-made collars, cuffs, straps, or bars. Even in some more mainstream stores, you'll find selections of bondage gear that are often combined into affordable starter packs.

around the house

Sex and shopping go together, certainly, but when it comes to getting playfully kinky, perhaps displaying your originality could be more impressive. Sure, you can go to a sex shop and invest in a closet's worth of kinky gear, but one look around your home when you're in the right frame of mind can yield up an armful of toys for your bondage arsenal.

When it comes to found objects, take care not to apply sticky duct tape directly to hairy skin (but stuck to old clothes are fine), and be aware that wooden rods and spoons, innocent though they may look, are far more painful than purpose-made corporal-punishment implements. The best policy is always to first test on yourself anything you've had an idea of using on your lover. Hairbrushes and soft-soled slippers, for example, are old favorites when it comes to establishing who wears the trousers around the house.

kissing with confidence

There are many types of kiss: dreamy, passive, harsh, probing, sloppy, warm, cool, passionate, or precise. For some, kissing is the most intimate act you can perform, while for all of us kissing is the gateway to what comes next. In fact, depending upon how it's done, there may or may not be a next.

Playful kissing games are one way for you and your partner to learn about each other's mouths and minds. At the beginning of a relationship, or when you have only kissed someone a few times, it's best to play it safe until you know what each other's tastes are. Never French-kiss as the first kiss in a series—build up to it. Kiss each other's lips ever so gently at first, just grazing them and pulling away slightly. Make your partner's lips long for yours. Tease them.

Take turns in taking the lead, as if you're ballroom dancing together. The partner who is following the other's lead should stay passive and responsive, copying their partner's kisses but not exceeding them in depth or intensity. Keep your tongue in your own mouth if they are kissing you with their lips, for example. Only this way will you find out how to deliver your partner an arousing kiss that will open up their sensual treasures to you.

food, romance, and aphrodisiacs

Food, intimacy, and sexual pleasure have always gone together, not least because a meal together is one of the few dates or celebratory occasions when—as opposed to being entertained—you can settle down together, talk, and anticipate (perhaps) the lovemaking to come.

Take care not to overdo it with rich sauces; if you're planning on sex, stick to high-protein but light foods (Japanese, Chinese, and Thai foods are quickly metabolized and full of energy). Researchers believe that commonly accepted aphrodisiacs such as asparagus and oysters have little effect, but that doesn't mean they're not sensual and fun. Meanwhile, there's some evidence for trying licorice, bananas, ginger, fennel, lettuce, and honey. Whatever their physical effects, sucking and swallowing some of these salty, spicy, even semen-like tastes can be pretty suggestive. But if applying to one another's bodies, take care around eyes—the tastier the food, the more it probably stings.

Bring a flush to your lover's cheeks by playing with things of different temperatures—from room temperature to freezing. Perhaps blindfold, even restrain them, and have them guess what the foods and fruits you produce for them are, from their smell, feel, and texture. You could even keep score. Wash food first, and trail it around your lover's body and genitals as part of your lovemaking.

liquid news—drinks and alcohol

While good sex and alcohol don't always mix, there's nothing like the sensation of champagne bubbles bursting on your skin to give you a sense of decadent sexuality, and the same fizzing feeling taken to your lover's genital flesh will give them an extra-special treat.

Dive between your lover's legs holding a mouthful of champagne or sparkling water. Take their genitals in your mouth or dribble it upon them. Take turns trading off the pleasure, say after a glass each. Alternatively, you could have plenty of fun getting sploshy with liquid foods on some plastic sheeting. At the right time, making a mess is liberating. Ice cream or chocolate spread are sensual treats that tease and torment your lover's flesh with differing temperatures, while giving you a tasty incentive to lick it all off.

oils and massage

You can give your lover a good rub without oils, but to add a bit of ritual, to signal that you're giving a relaxing massage, oils are, well, essential. You need a greasy, slippery skin surface if you want to reach your partner's knotted, tense muscles without causing friction burns to the skin. It's great, too, if your lover is hairy or fleshy. Baby oil or cosmetic oils are fine, while your best option is a neutral massage oil—such as peach nut—which can be mixed with essential oils of your choice. Most essential oils should never touch the skin undiluted, as some can be powerfully caustic. And, of course, warm anything you use between your hands first.

Alternatively, burn these aromatherapy oils in an oil burner. Good smells have great effects when your lover's relaxed and breathing deeply, and will really give them the impression you know what you're doing. Avoid essential oils altogether if there's even a chance that you or your partner might be pregnant. Otherwise, oils of lavender, eucalyptus, basil, and bergamot, along with rose, sandalwood, neroli (orange blossom), and ylang ylang, are mood enhancers and reputedly aphrodisiac.

Make sure you are clear whether you're giving an arousing, foreplay massage or a truly relaxing experience after which nothing is expected of your lover but to stay in the relaxed space you've created. Few things will be more annoying for both of you than finding you've confused these goals. If you're taking the latter option, remove all mental pressures and, whether with long, gliding strokes, or kneading and squeezing ones, let them empty their minds of everything but sensation.

thrills

teases and tantra

★ If possible, save your bedroom for sleeping and making love. If you use the room regularly to work, watch television, or do the ironing, you'll find it hard not to let these things enter your mind as you make love there.

★ Take turns stroking and gently rubbing the bases of each other's spines—you'll both feel warm about each other.

★ Women, if you think your man's not far from orgasm, cup his testicles evenly and gently pull them downwards. Men, you can do this for yourselves, too. Try it when you're masturbating. A man's balls retract *towards the shaft of the penis before ejaculation, so this can delay matters.*

★ *Regular exercise of the P.C. muscles will make women tighter and men last longer. If you're not sure where they are, imagine you're trying not to urinate—it's the area that will be contracting. Gently squeeze and relax it repeatedly whenever it occurs to you—a perfectly invisible exercise you can do at your desk at work.*

★ *Harness the power of your imagination when you're making love. For fantasy, sure, but also for empathy. Think about how it might physically feel to have the other sex's genitals, and think about the sensations your actions are causing your lover to have. Imagine what it feels like to receive the strokes you are administering.*

safe sex and erotica

Sexual-health scares have made us more aware of non-penetrative erotic activities. Think about enjoying some erotica or pornography as you mutually masturbate. Otherwise, for safe sex, condoms that conform to international safety standards are essential unless you are both absolutely sure you have a clean bill of sexual health. The inconvenience of condoms is a small price to pay for peace of mind. In fact, regular sex boosts the immune system, so safe sex is better for you than no sex. Be sure to continue the sexual contact, touching and eye contact, in order to avoid that dreaded pause while you put on a condom.

Even better, make a point of incorporating condoms into your lovemaking; make it a positively sensual act of foreplay. Women, caress your lover as he puts on a condom; help him not to wilt.

Or put it on for him. Don't rip the wrapper with your teeth: hold the condom by the teat to squeeze out the air and roll it down his shaft as you gently squeeze the base of his penis. Make a ring with the thumb and index finger of your other hand, to keep it upright, erect, and to ensure the condom goes on safely.

Make sure the condom is fully unrolled, so that he can grab the end at the base of his penis with his fingers and hold it in place when it's time to withdraw. Don't use them with oil-based lubes, of course. For an adventurous, naughty, professional touch, try putting it on with your mouth. Be careful to cover your teeth with your lips, in order not to tear the Latex. Avoid oily lipstick, balm, or lip-gloss. With a little practice, this will give him a super-sensual sensation that'll mean he'll never see using condoms as a chore again.

index